Crimson Clover

A small bouquet of ponderings

Danae Cornish

BookLeaf Publishing

India | USA | UK

Copyright © Danae Cornish

All Rights Reserved.

This book has been self-published with all reasonable efforts taken to make the material error-free by the author. No part of this book shall be used, reproduced in any manner whatsoever without written permission from the author, except in the case of brief quotations embodied in critical articles and reviews.

The Author of this book is solely responsible and liable for its content including but not limited to the views, representations, descriptions, statements, information, opinions, and references ["Content"]. The Content of this book shall not constitute or be construed or deemed to reflect the opinion or expression of the Publisher or Editor. Neither the Publisher nor Editor endorse or approve the Content of this book or guarantee the reliability, accuracy, or completeness of the Content published herein and do not make any representations or warranties of any kind, express or implied, including but not limited to the implied warranties of merchantability, fitness for a particular purpose.

The Publisher and Editor shall not be liable whatsoever...

Made with ❤ on the BookLeaf Publishing Platform

www.bookleafpub.in

www.bookleafpub.com

Dedication

To a braver me,
and whomever she's given to love.

Preface

For You will not leave my soul in Sheol

~ psalm 16:10a

Acknowledgements

Thanks to my brother Matthew for being my library buddy, and (mostly) not minding the light while I work late. Thanks to Amy Bender for coffee on the most snowy of days; Your conversation is still giving energy and warmth. Others contributed vast amounts to these now mild efforts of mine: my parents, brothers, teachers, friends. May the beauty they've poured out return a hundred fold.

2 Corinthians 9:8

I will not fear I have no good to give;
If you are with me,
My hand is always full
To bless.

Genesis 15

I do not have,
to hold or own,
the substance of your word.
Here wanders through the promised land
a nomad of the earth;
I lack all proof to see or show
this story will give birth.

I am an old man
with an old wife;
Shepherd who can't speak,
Prophet without hope,
Warrior feeling weak.
I am a virgin still
locked inside a tower,
Your friend, Lord, weeping for her brother
as he rots inside the tomb
of aching earth,

the broken womb
of dust outside of Eden.

Hegai

There is some sort of
waiting on your Word
that you reward,

some kind of patient ache,
that you relieve
for your name's sake,

some hope that aspires
to intertwine my heart
with yours, Oh God,
which you desire.

But then there is another
fire, pride that won't be soothed.
Seeking saving for the self,
too late, too fake, too cruel.

What does righteous fear
dare to ask you for?
How can I dress this emptiness
in such a way
that you accept my petition?

Shalom Shalom Shalom

It's a hello to the brokennes-
Good tidings sent to bless.
It's a knowing things won't always stay
in this state of unrest.

Purple Falls

Put that ache to good use
Go grab your hat and boots.
Come with me; we'll look up at the stars.

Throw your arms up, when your
running down the stairs
or find yourself in an empty
isle of the grocery strore
Spill your heart into the air.

Breathe deep when in a sea of strangers
That air of needing something
someplace else;
Eyes locked, or searching,
Too shy or serious,
or sad
to stop and notice that

there is always darkness
and space
and the black hole of the silent song
that wants to be sung-
Love ever always being love.

Mystery

Eyes, Word,
Tomb,Star;
All His heart
is
near and far.

Your Book

Maybe don't be afraid
That your story is scattered out
Across so many places: highways, feilds
and kitchens
Countries far, hearts of those you've missed for long;
The notebook on your phone,
sketch pad, planner, calendar,
reciepts, checks and sticky notes,
air above the walking paths,
cemetery dirt.

David said
his days- they all were written before one came to be.

And yet

You think it would be healing,
that apology on a page -
Not soft spoken once
in a sterile space,
Expected to be digested as quick as it was said.

Perhaps, yes.

You think it would help
to wrap the wound in wisdom words
after rinsing it long in
clearest truth
regardless of the hurt.

Maybe so,
maybe so.

The Darkest Light

That's the strange thing-
Every color's here;

Paradox all shimmering
Pinciples so clear.

The cross, the cross
Vortex of all time.
You'll never know a thing in truth
before it's set beside
This.

Meet

You have made me finite, limited,
and in frustration, I find this means
I must have a specific purpose.

For I cannot serve all things in every way.
I cannot love all men the same.
Humility grips me with a death grasp-
I gasp for understanding.
I wonder who told me, anyways,
that I wouldn't have to die,
that goodbye could be a
more than bygone byword.

I'll spit out the fruit
of needing to be just like you
and choose
to need you instead;

Infinite, Unlimited-
my hunger will be met.

Done

Righteousness
not by my decision
but by your submission
not by my will
but you, giving up yours.

Where The Soil is Dark

Scapegoat. Another dull sermon,
the same podium.
Blinds closed,
I think I already know

Surprises as the airplanes weave
Hope rising at odd angles
Senses dull to what is ought
So many doors are tangled.
My mind is clogged with questions,
and Moses died on the Mountain

And the ram was caught in the thicket,
And the knife was caught in the air.
And these questions won't stop knocking in my brain
Sometimes it's right
To send a child away.

Fall with me

Here in it, with me
you are
not so outside or
tomorrow
looking down and through and then

you are not puzzling like me, are you?

my thoughts go to float;
my room
is alone
though i'm in it.

Turn me inside out—
maybe that would do it.

Just Wondering

What is it about idols that he hates?

Something that stands in sacred
place, that pushes light away;
takes the highest crown and seat, feigns
your shining face.

Does he hate it when we cry out
to stone ears and wooden eyes,
when we mistake the made thing
for having powers sole divine

Do you hate it when we turn
to the breathless to breath prayers,
hate the way we become dull
and deaf
and dumb
and still.

Is it possible,
I pray too much
but to another god;
How do I know the one I beg
Is God, Is God, Is God?

Author

All the time
unseen
Till you shine
the space to breathe;
Sing the land out from the sea.

A Noonday Rose

I now know
a beautiful, wonderful
secret:
That Kelli lives
on the other side of
that grey wall, and a
lighthouse picture hangs beside her desk.
Her eyes are alive
and real and January 8th
is not her birthday.

Tuesday

Your silence slices through
the dam I built up tall -
the shakey shrine to my own gods of right and wrong.
The small wind of your Spirit
makes it fall.
You hide me in the mid of rock,
and roll the entrance shut.
You hide from me
and me from you
and wait
till I am blind enough to hear,
deaf enough to see.
Maybe, if you had been here
I would have never known
your glory.

C.H.A.N.G.E.

Come,
Humbly
Accept
New
Grace
Everyday.

Cosmic Prism

God has not sent
His word
to us to break,
and cannot mend,
But has fulfilled
the Law in Christ
and resurrected him.

1 John 3:2

If you dress
the sky in living color;
Awake the world in wonder,
What will you do in me?
Oh how I long
to be clothed,
not unclothed.
Oh how I long to know
as I'm known.

Made To See

You saw me when
I looked away,
followed when I turned.
You ate up all the pain of space
that I made when I spurned
your life;
you died.
Yet in the farness of a tomb,
you drew a breath
to fill my lungs anew.

www.ingramcontent.com/pod-product-compliance
Lightning Source LLC
LaVergne TN
LVHW010849200726
843508LV00012B/2822